Bible Jumbo
Coloring & Activity Book

bendon®

The BENDON name, logo and
Tear and Share are trademarks of
Bendon, Inc., Ashland, OH 44805.

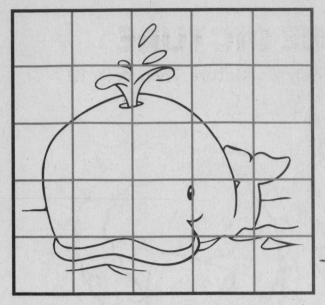

Use the grid below to draw the picture.

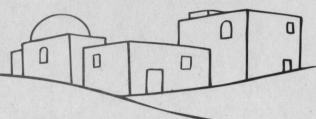

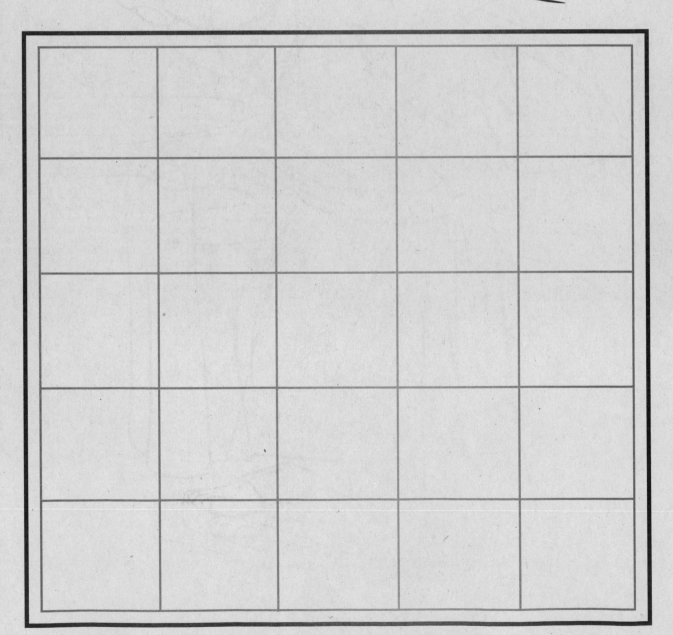

FINISH THE PICTURE

Trace the gray lines to finish the picture. Then, color it!

UNSCRAMBLE THE BIBLE WORDS

Write your answer on the line below each word.

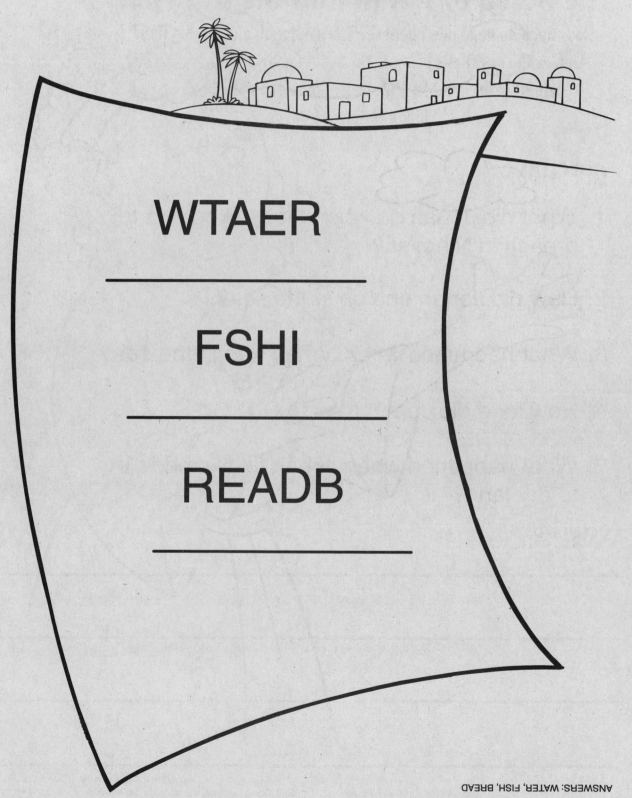

WTAER

_____

FSHI

_____

READB

_____

BIBLE QUIZ
The story of Jonah and the Big Fish

How much do you know about the story of Jonah and the big fish? Answer the questions below to the best of your ability. It may be helpful to use a Bible. The story of Jonah is in the book of Jonah chapters 1-4.

QUESTIONS:

1. What did Jonah do when God asked him to preach in Ninevah?

2. How did Jonah end up in the sea?

3. What happened when Jonah was in the sea?

4. How long did Jonah pray to God?

5. What happened when Jonah finally made it to dry land?

ANSWERS:

_____

_____

_____

_____

ANSWERS:
1. He went in the opposite direction. 2. He was thrown overboard. 3. He was swallowed by a big fish.
4. 3 days and 3 nights 5. He went and preached in Ninevah.

FINISH THE PICTURE

Trace the gray lines to finish the picture. Then, color it!

UNSCRAMBLE THE BIBLE WORDS

Write your answer on the line below each word.

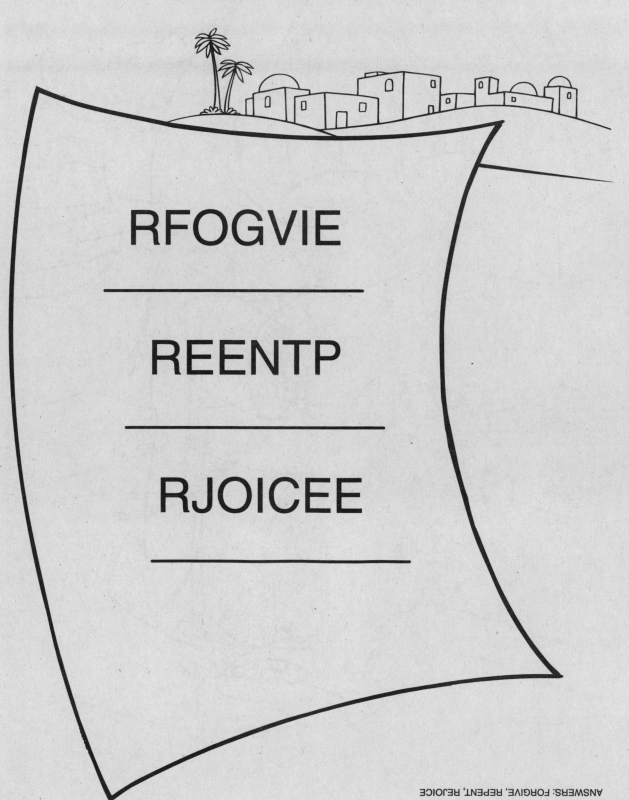

RFOGVIE

_____

REENTP

_____

RJOICEE

_____

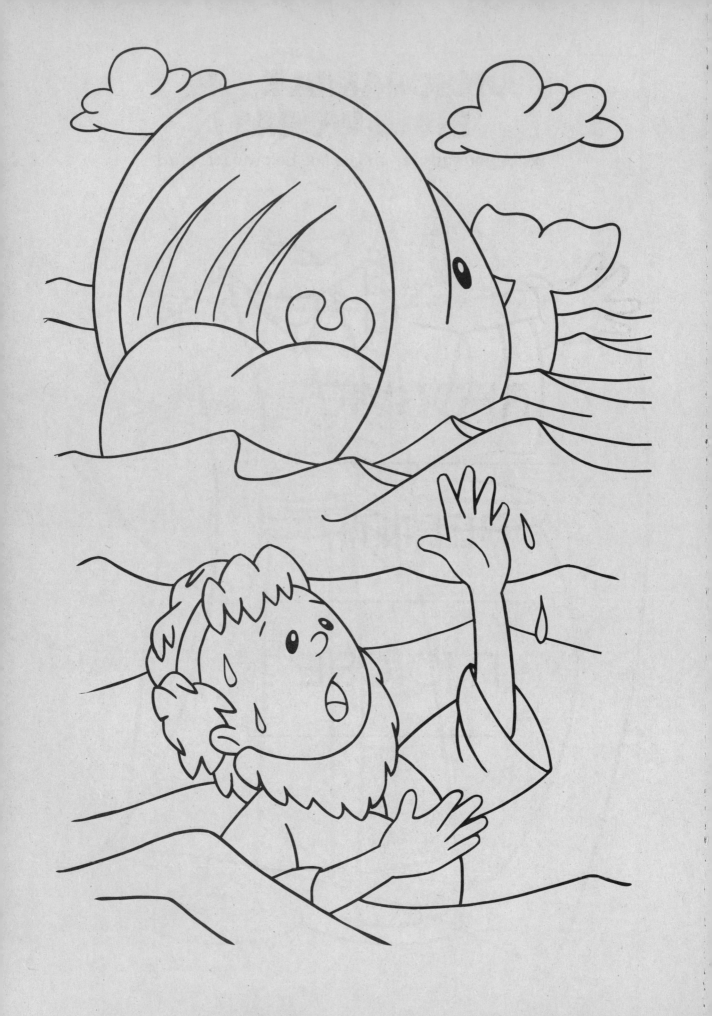

BIBLE QUIZ
The story of Joseph

How much do you know about the story of Joseph?
Answer the questions below to the best of your ability. It may be
helpful to use a Bible. The story of Joseph is in the book of
Genesis chapters 37-50.

QUESTIONS:

1. Who was Joseph's father?

2. True/False. Joseph was the favorite of twelve sons.

3. What happened as a result of Joseph's brothers jealousy?

4. How did Joseph become the governor of Eygpt?

5. True/False. Joseph and his father never reunite.

ANSWERS:

_____

_____

_____

_____

BIBLE TIC-TAC-TOE

Use the grid below to draw the picture.

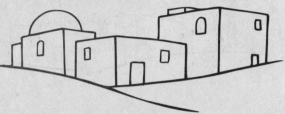

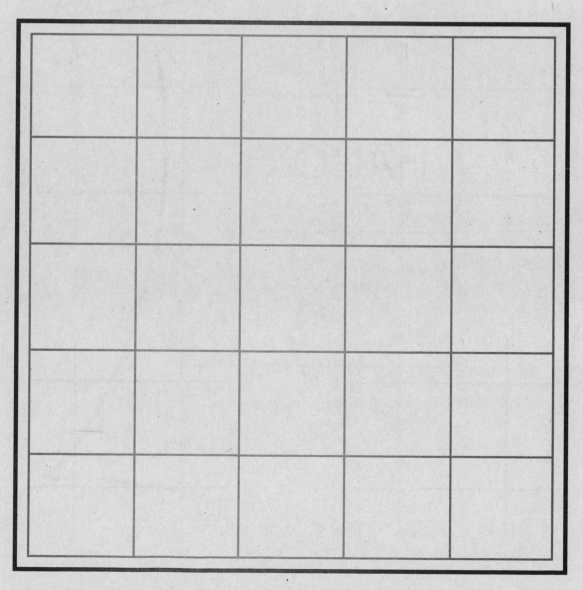

UNSCRAMBLE THE BIBLE WORDS

Write your answer on the line below each word.

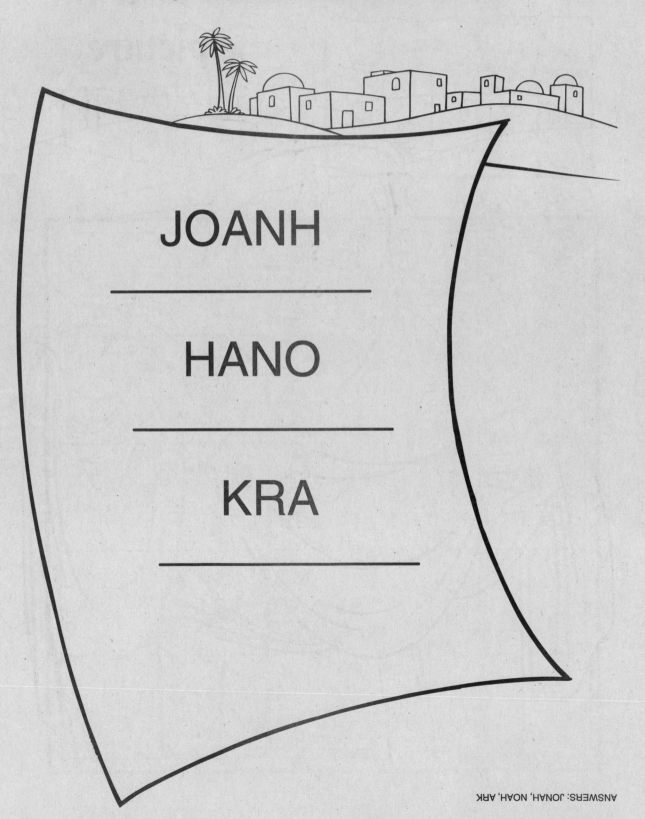

JOANH

_____

HANO

_____

KRA

_____

What is your
FAVORITE BIBLE STORY?

Draw or write your answer in the space below.

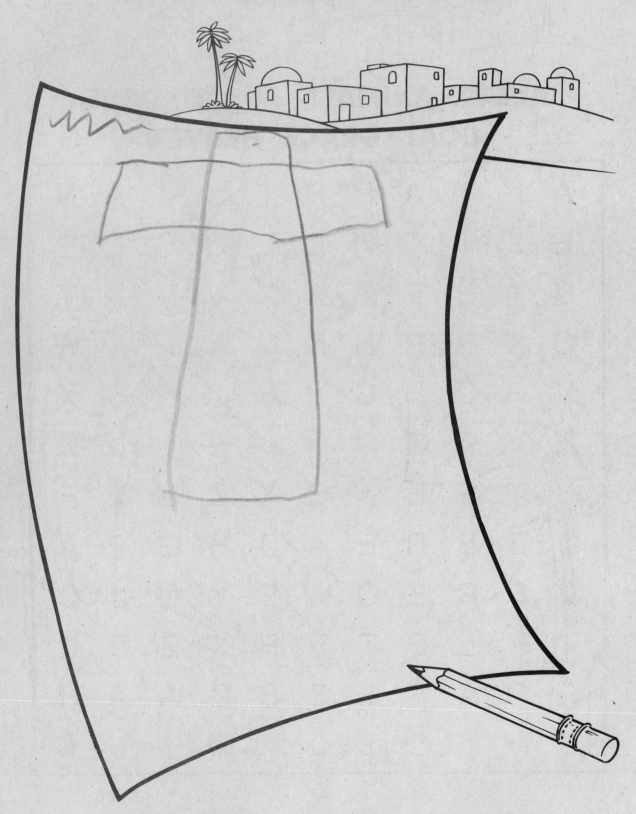

WORD SEARCH

Find and circle the words in the puzzle.

ALTAR · ANIMALS · BREAD · DOVE
GOAT · GRACE · HEAVEN

```
A L T A R R T U J A N
F J I T H E L O C E E
D I R T N Z X V V V Y Y
O K S P H N G A F L W
V R C H C L E O N C X
E V A Z D H V E I J G
Y T E E W Q X Z M E R
I J B R E A D H G P A
J F R E Q W B Y U J C
I K L P T P R X Z D E
G O A T L S S E W A H
S W F G S L A M I N A
```

Use the grid below to draw the picture.

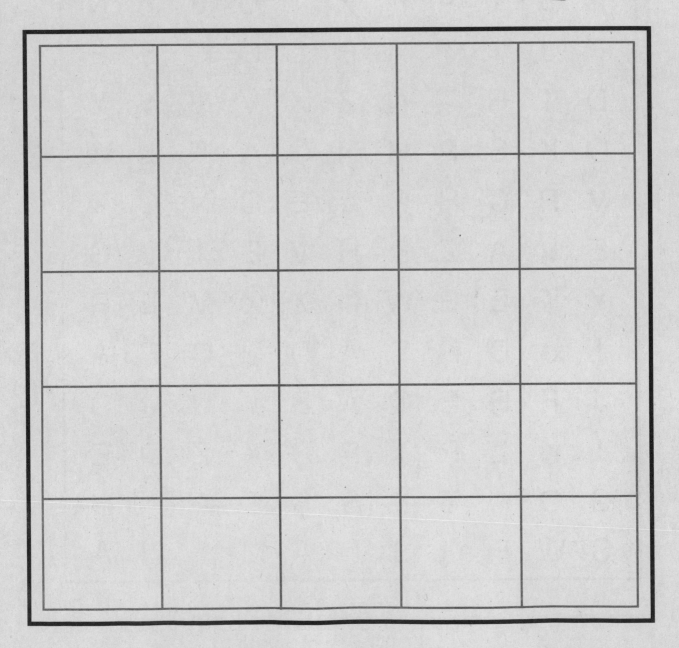

BIBLE QUIZ
The story of Baby Jesus

How much do you know about the story of baby Jesus? Answer the questions below to the best of your ability. It may be helpful to use a Bible. The story of Jesus is in the book of Luke 1: 26-32, and Luke 2: 1-7.

QUESTIONS:

1. Who came to Mary to tell her she would have a baby?

2. True/False. The baby will be the son of God.

3. Who was Mary's husband to be?

4. Where did Mary give birth?

5. Who came to see baby Jesus?

ANSWERS:

_____

_____

_____

_____

ANSWERS:
1. an angel, 2. True, 3. Joesph, 4. In a manger, 5. shepherds and wise men.

FINISH THE PICTURE

Trace the gray lines to finish the picture. Then, color it!

UNSCRAMBLE THE BIBLE WORDS

Write your answer on the line below each word.

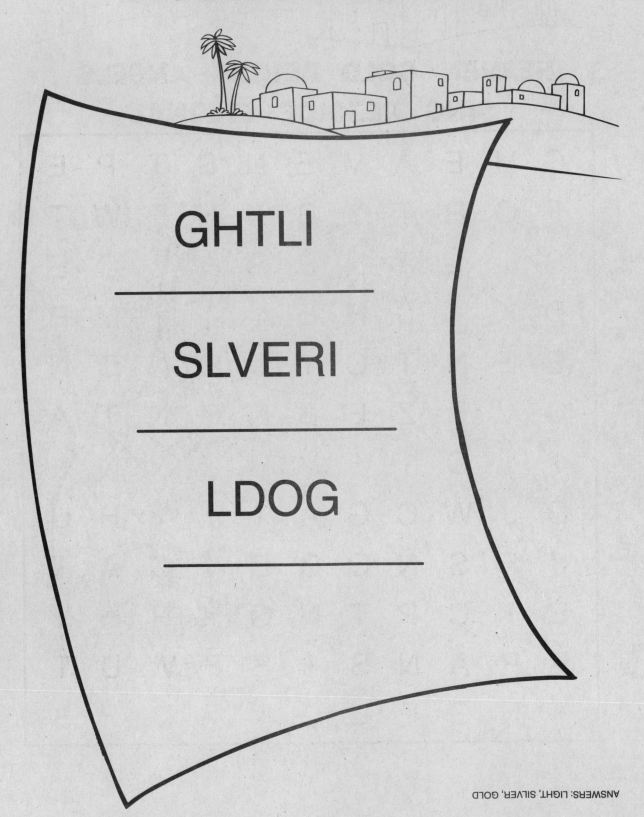

GHTLI

_____

SLVERI

_____

LDOG

_____

WORD SEARCH
Find and circle the words in the puzzle.

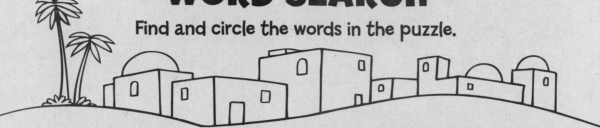

HEAVEN · GOLD · BRIGHT · ANGELS
SING · REJOICE · ETERNAL

```
G H E A V E N S T P E
F O R T Y B X H R W T
S I L T N B R H O O E
D K I D H E Y L F M R
E E N T C Y G O N O N
C V B Z E B N G N T A
I T O I I V R K N N L
O J W C G A I I I H U
J F S N Q G B V G A I
E I C P T N O X R H V
R P A N S I S F W U T
A N G E L S N Y B R S
```

Use the grid below to draw the picture.

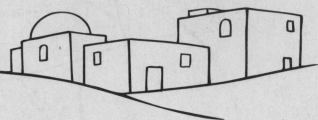

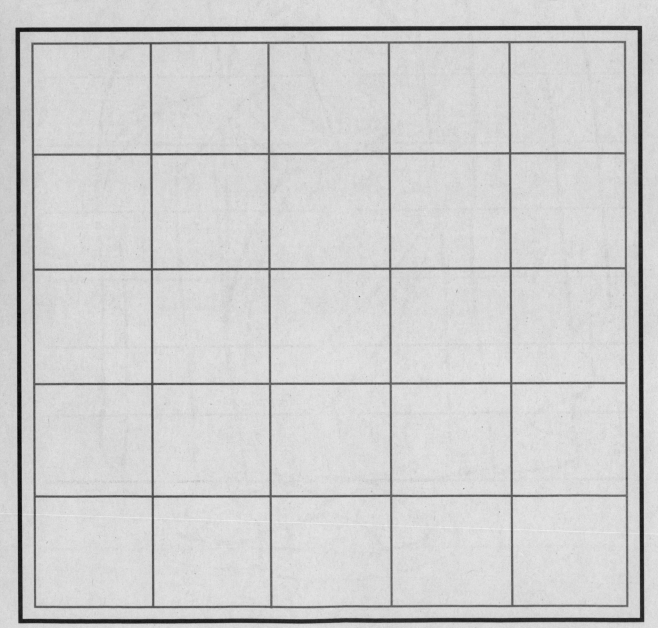

How many words can you make using the letters in
TESTAMENT?

_____   _____

_____   _____

_____   _____

_____   _____

_____   _____

_____   _____

_____   _____

WORD SEARCH

Find and circle the words in the puzzle.

KING · SEA · SAINT · PRAYER
RAINBOW · MARY · SILVER · STARS

```
A P T E R R T U J A S
F J I M A R Y O C E I
G I R T N Z X V A Y L
N K S P H N G A F L V
I R C H W L E O N C E
K V A Z K O N G I J R
Y T E E W Q B Z M E R
I J B O F A D N G P A
J F R E Q W B Y I J C
I K L P R A Y E R A E
G N L T L S S E W A R
S T A R S L T N I A S
```

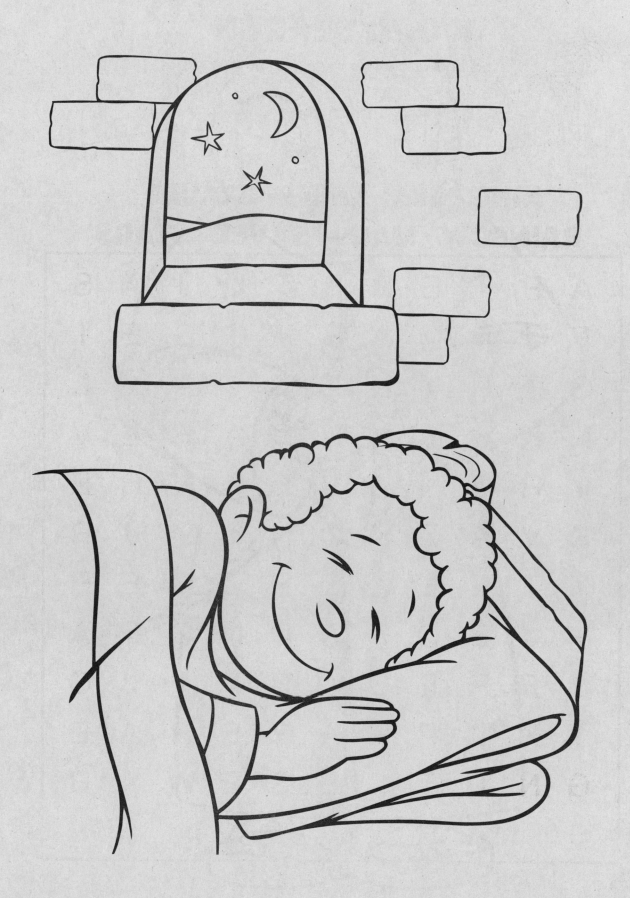

Help Mary find her way to Bethlehem.

Start

Finish

Which picture is different?

1.

2.

3.

4.

ANSWER: 2

BIBLE QUIZ
The story of Noah's Ark

How much do you know about the story of Noah and his ark? Answer the questions below to the best of your ability. It may be helpful to use a Bible. The story of Noah is in the book of Genesis chapters 6,7, and 8, and chapter 9 verses 1-17.

QUESTIONS:

1. Who told Noah to build an ark?

2. True/False. God sent two of every animal to Noah to put on the ark.

3. How long did it rain?

4. What did God send as a sign that the rains would never again destroy the earth?

ANSWERS:

_____

_____

_____

_____

FINISH THE PICTURE

Trace the gray lines to finish the picture. Then, color it!

UNSCRAMBLE THE BIBLE WORDS

Write your answer on the line below each word.

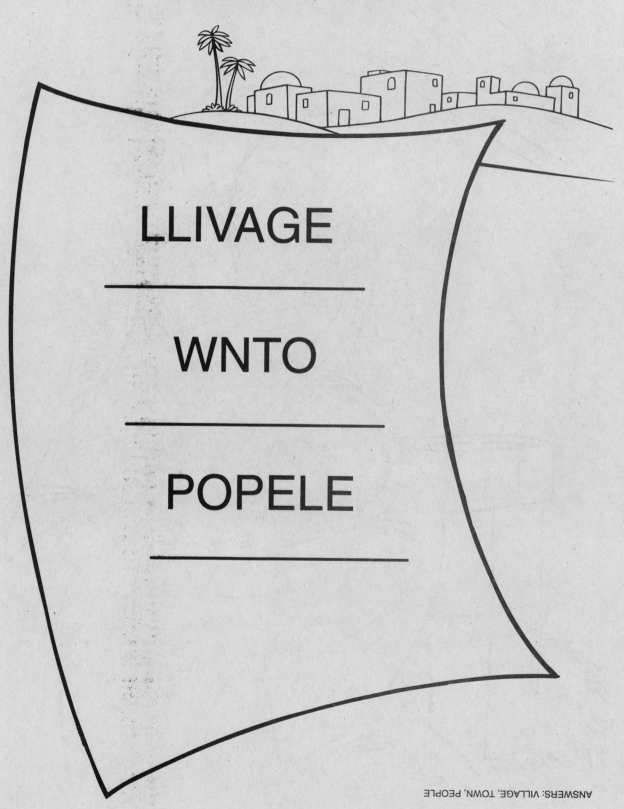

LLIVAGE

_____

WNTO

_____

POPELE

_____

BIBLE TIC-TAC-TOE

WORD SEARCH

Find and circle the words in the puzzle.

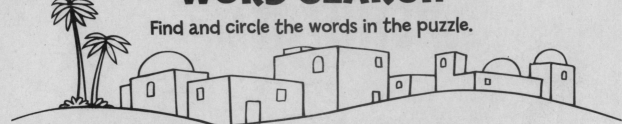

JOSEPH · BROTHERS · PHARAOH
GOVERNOR · EGYPT · COAT

```
J  A  L  B  R  R  K  T  A  O  C
F  O  M  I  A  Y  M  Z  R  G  H
G  I  S  T  N  B  X  D  A  O  A
O  K  S  E  H  N  Y  L  F  V  L
B  R  C  T  P  Y  G  E  N  E  M
R  V  A  Z  K  H  N  G  I  R  R
O  T  E  E  I  V  Z  Z  M  N  R
T  J  B  C  A  A  D  X  G  O  X
H  F  S  N  Q  W  B  Y  M  R  E
E  I  C  P  T  P  R  X  Z  A  G
R  P  A  N  S  S  S  E  W  A  U
S  I  A  R  P  H  A  R  A  O  H
```

How many words can you make using the letters in
BETHLEHEM?

_____   _____

_____   _____

_____   _____

_____   _____

_____   _____

_____   _____

_____   _____

WORD SEARCH

Find and circle the words in the puzzle.

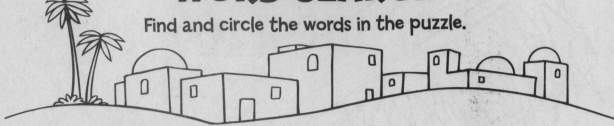

OCEAN · LAMB · DISCIPLE · FIG
FIRE · FAMILY · PSALMS · RAIN

```
L A M B R R T U J A P
F A M I L Y Y O C E S
G I R T N Z X V A Y A
K K S P H N G E F L L
V R C H W L L O N C M
K V A Z K P N G I J S
Y T E E I N B Z M E R
I J B C A A D N G I F
J F S E Q W B Y I J I
I I C P T P R X Z A R
D O A T L S S E W A E
N I A R S L T N I A S
```

FINISH THE PICTURE

Trace the gray lines to finish the picture. Then, color it!

Use the grid below to draw the picture.

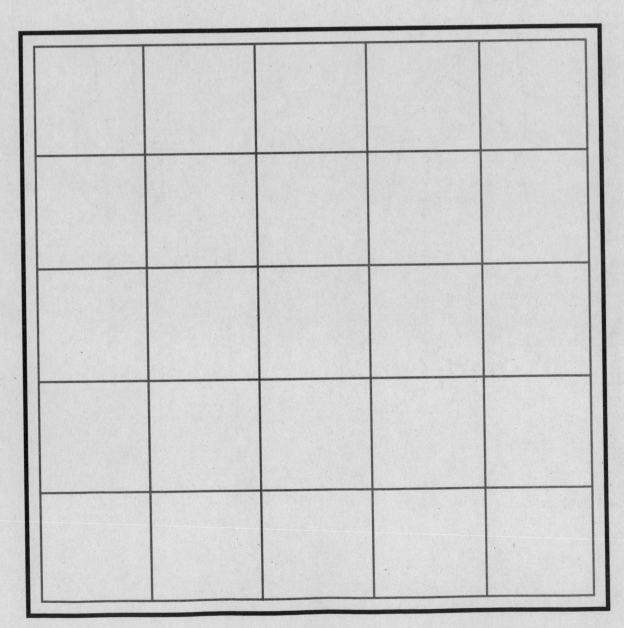

UNSCRAMBLE THE BIBLE WORDS

Write your answer on the line below each word.

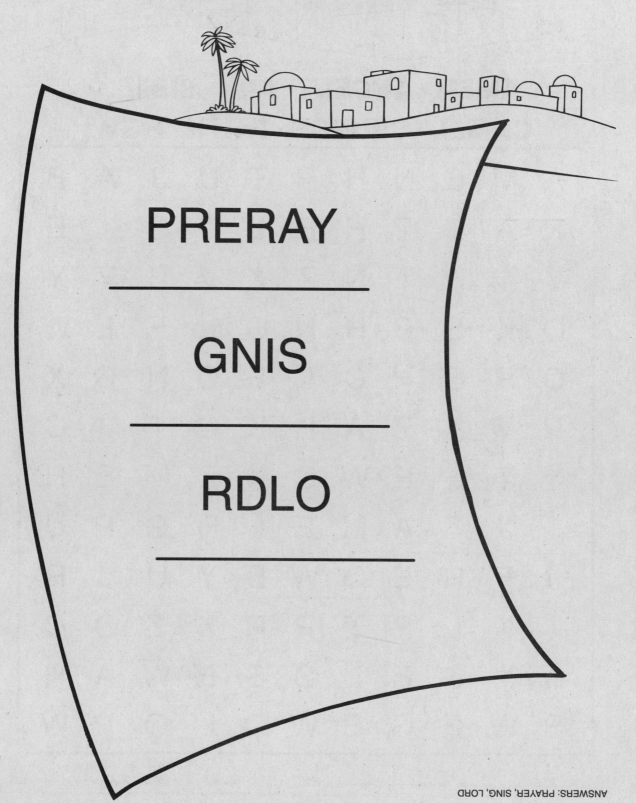

PRERAY

_____

GNIS

_____

RDLO

_____

WORD SEARCH

Find and circle the words in the puzzle.

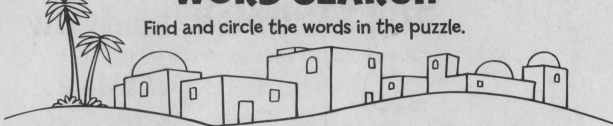

AMEN · ANGELS · ARK · BIBLE
CAMEL · CHURCH · FAITH · FISH

```
A M E N H R T U J A B
F A I T H E L O C I E
Y I R T N Z X V B Y Y
O K S P H N G L F L W
C R C H C L E O N C X
N V A Z A R K O I J C
Y T E E W Q X Z M E H
I J C A M E L H G P U
J F R E Q W B Y U J R
I K L P T P R X Z D C
A N G E L S S E W A H
S W F G E W Q L O P W
```

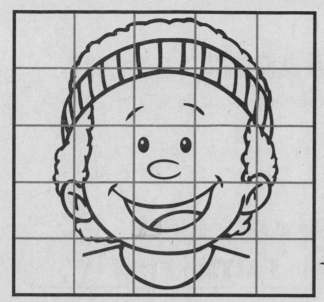

Use the grid below to draw the picture.

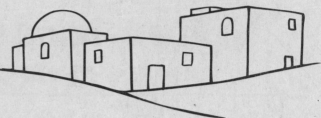

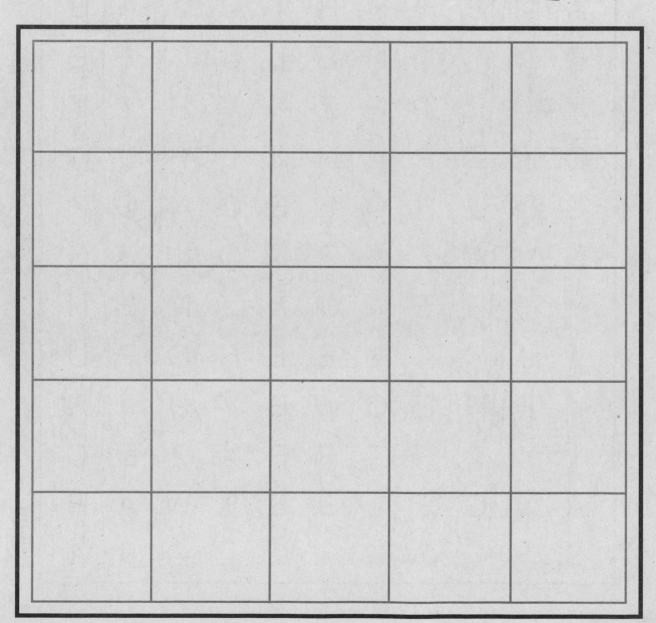

Which picture is different?

1.

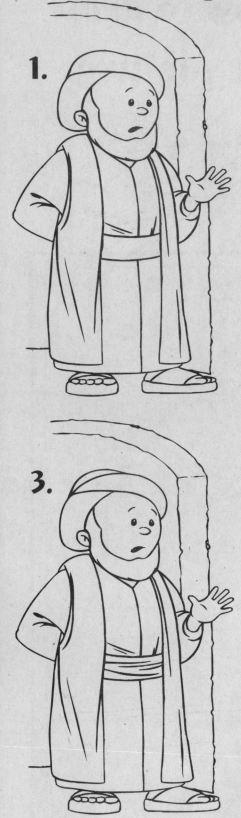

3.

4.

ANSWER: 1

WORD SEARCH

Find and circle the words in the puzzle.

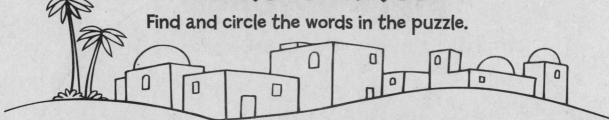

ARK · ANIMALS · TWO · RAIN
FORTY · SURVIVE · RAINBOW

```
J A N I M A L S T P T
F O R T Y B X H R W O
S I A T N B R H O O N
D K I T H E Y L F M L
C E N T C Y G O N O E
D V B Z E H N G N T R
X T O I I V Z K N N R
T J W C G A I X I H U
R F S N Q R B V A A I
S I C P T P O X R K V
B P A N S S S F W U B
A R K M P B N Y B R S
```

UNSCRAMBLE THE BIBLE WORDS

Write your answer on the line below each word.

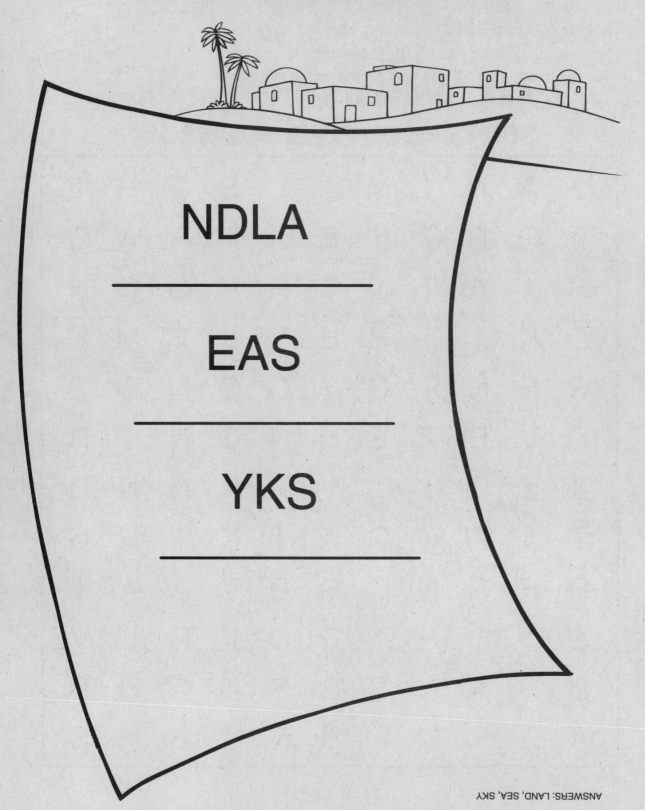

NDLA

_____

EAS

_____

YKS

_____

BIBLE SQUARES

Taking turns, connect a line from one COW to another. Whoever makes the line that completes a box puts his or her initial inside the box. The person with the most squares at the end of the game wins!

EXAMPLE

WORD SEARCH

Find and circle the words in the puzzle.

SEA · JONAH · PREACH · WHALE
THREE · PRAY · LAND · FORGIVE

```
J A L B R R K T T P W
F O P R E A C H R G H
L I F T N B R D A O A
A K S T H E Y L F M L
N E C T E Y G O N O E
D V V Z K H N G N T R
X T E I I V Z K M N R
T J B C G A E X G H G
R F S N Q R B Y M A I
S I C P T P O X Z N F
E P A N S S S F W O T
A R A M P R A Y B J S
```

UNSCRAMBLE THE BIBLE WORDS

Write your answer on the line below each word.

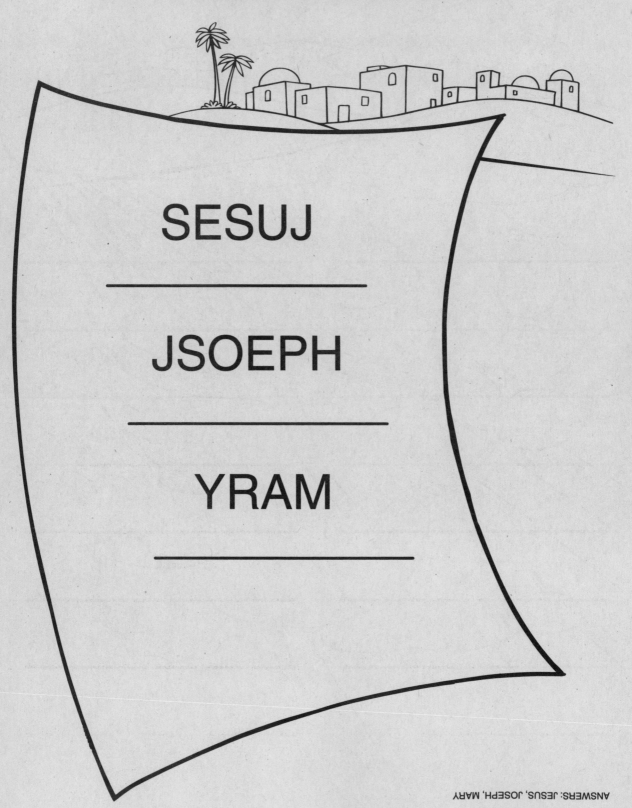

SESUJ
_____

JSOEPH
_____

YRAM
_____

How many words can you make using the letters in
ANGELS IN HEAVEN?

_____   _____

_____   _____

_____   _____

_____   _____

_____   _____

_____   _____

_____   _____

WORD SEARCH

Find and circle the words in the puzzle.

MARY · BABY · MANGER · STRAW
DONKEY · GIFTS · LORD

```
J  A  L  B  R  R  K  T  D  P  C
F  O  M  A  N  G  E  R  R  G  H
S  I  F  T  N  B  O  D  A  O  A
T  K  S  T  H  L  Y  L  F  M  D
R  R  C  T  X  Y  G  O  N  O  M
A  V  A  Z  K  H  N  G  N  T  R
W  T  E  E  I  V  Z  K  M  N  R
T  J  B  C  A  A  E  X  G  L  G
R  F  S  N  Q  Y  B  Y  M  R  I
X  I  C  P  T  P  B  X  Z  A  F
Z  P  A  N  S  S  S  A  W  A  T
Y  R  A  M  P  H  K  M  B  T  S
```

Matching

Find the two pictures that are exactly the same.

UNSCRAMBLE THE BIBLE WORDS

Write your answer on the line below each word.

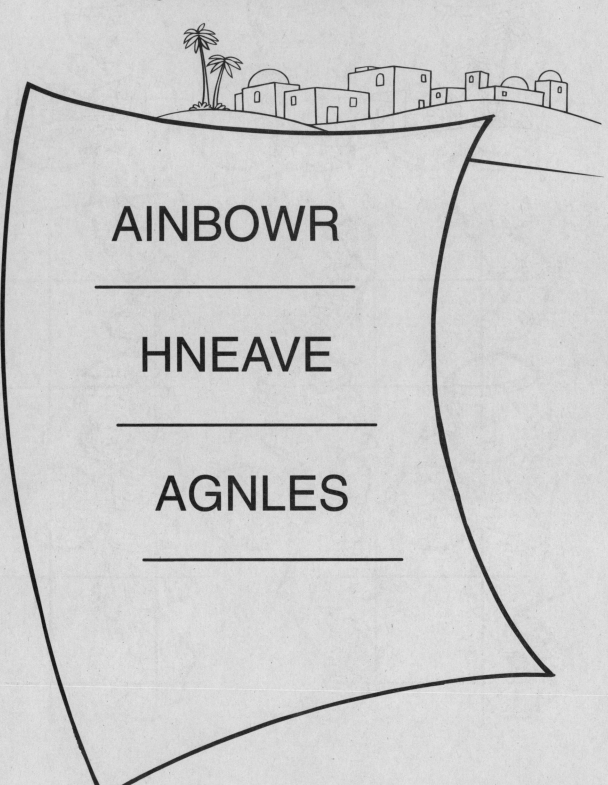

AINBOWR

_____

HNEAVE

_____

AGNLES

_____

BIBLE TIC-TAC-TOE

Use the grid below to draw the picture.

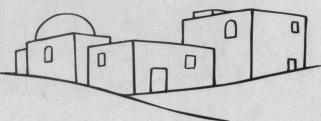

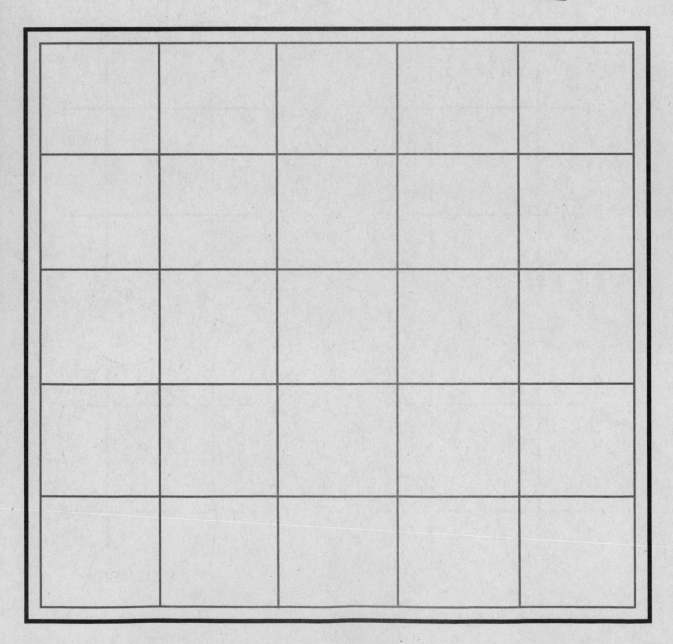

Which picture is different?

1.

2.

3.

4.

5.

BIBLE SQUARES

Taking turns, connect a line from one DOVE to another. Whoever makes the line that completes a box puts his or her initial inside the box. The person with the most squares at the end of the game wins!

EXAMPLE

UNSCRAMBLE THE BIBLE WORDS

Write your answer on the line below each word.

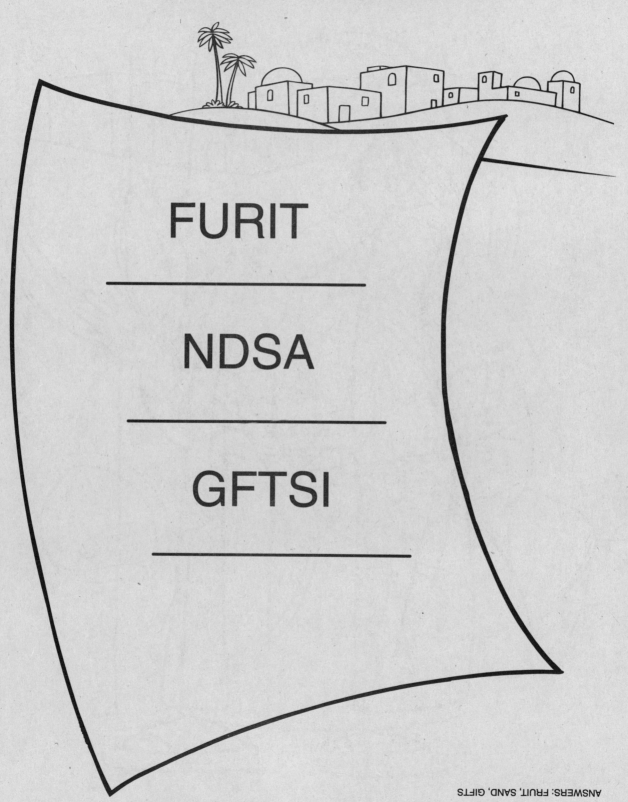

FURIT

_____

NDSA

_____

GFTSI

_____

How many words can you make using the letters in
JONAH AND THE FISH?

WORD SEARCH

Find and circle the words in the puzzle.

**JESUS · BABY · BETHLEHEM · NIGHT
STARS · GOLD · MYRRH**

```
B A L B R R N I G H T
F E M I A Y M Y R R H
G I T T N B X D A Y A
O K S H H N Y L F L L
P R C H L L L O N C M
L V A Z K E N G I J R
Y T E E I N H Z M E R
I J B C A A D E G I J
J F S E Q W B Y M J E
I I C P T P R X Z A S
S T A R S S S S E W A U
N I A R S L T N I A S
```

Children's Bedtime Prayer

Now I lay me down to sleep,
I pray the Lord my soul to keep:
May God guard me through the night
And wake me with the morning light.
Amen.

--- *Traditional*